PROFESSOR ZACH'S
K-5 MATH
CURRICULUM

PROFESSOR ZACH'S K-5 MATH CURRICULUM

ZACHARIYA TRICHAS

iUniverse®

PROFESSOR ZACH'S K-5 MATH CURRICULUM

iUniverse books may be ordered through booksellers or by contacting:

iUniverse
1663 Liberty Drive
Bloomington, IN 47403
www.iuniverse.com
1-800-Authors (1-800-288-4677)

ISBN: 978-1-5320-5834-9 (sc)
ISBN: 978-1-5320-5835-6 (e)

Print information available on the last page.

iUniverse rev. date: 10/10/2018

I dedicate this book to my parents and my math teachers, Mr. Joujan and Mr. Buckley, because I couldn't have done it without them.

میں اس کتاب کو اپنے والدین اور میرے ریاضی اساتذہ، مسٹر جوجن اور مسٹر بکل کو وقف کرتا ہوں کیونکہ میں ان کی حمایت اور رہنمائی کے بغیر ایسا نہیں کرسکتا.

ADDITION

Learning Objectives:

⮕ Students will be able to add together two one-digit numbers

Introduction:

⮕ Show students the diagram on slide two

⮕ Draw a "before addition" diagram on the board, illustrating two cars as one group, and a single car as another

⮕ Draw the corresponding "after addition" diagram next to it, showing both groups combined with three cars together

⮕ Ask students to count the cars before and after

⮕ Take responses from students
⮕ Reveal the correct answer, write the corresponding equation underneath the diagrams, and explain the process of addition

Guided Practice:

⮕ Students will be given an addition worksheet, and the class will do the first few problems together on the blackboard
⮕ Using illustrations, the teacher will relate the problems from the worksheet to the problem from the slideshow. The teacher may also allow students to count on their fingers to determine an answer

Independent Work:

⮕ Students will work in small groups, solving equations from the worksheet
⮕ Once students master single digit addition, double and triple digit addition will be introduced, using column addition as a teaching method

Subtraction

Learning Objectives:

- Students will be able to subtract two one-digit numbers

Introduction:

- Show students the diagram on slide 12
- Draw a diagram of the two groups of candy
- Instead of adding the two, put a subtraction symbol between them
- To illustrate subtraction, cross one piece of candy off from each side until the side that is subtracting reaches zero
- Use slide 13's number line to further illustrate how the original value of four has decreased by two

Guided Practice:

- Students will be given a subtraction worksheet, and the class will do the first problem together on the board
- Using Illustrations, the teacher will relate the problems from the worksheet to the problem from the slideshow

Independent Work:

- Students will work in small groups, solving equations from the worksheet

- Once students master single digit subtraction, work on double- and triple-digit subtraction

MULTIPLICATION

Learning Objectives:

⮕ Students will be able to multiply two one-digit numbers

Introduction:

⮕ Show students diagram on slide 20
⮕ Reveal that multiplication is the same as repeated addition as shown on slide 21
⮕ Use the same grouping method that was used in the addition lesson to illustrate this fact
⮕ Have students use the method of repeated addition until they are comfortable with memorizing multiplication tables

Guided Practice:

⮕ The class will work through a few problems as the teacher demonstrates that multiplication is repeated addition

Independent Work:

⮕ Students will go through the single digit multiplication worksheet, using the repeated addition method initially to understand multiplication, after significant practice, have students try to do multiplication without using addition, instead using the multiplication symbol in the column method

DIVISION

Learning Objectives:

➲ Students will be able to divide two one-digit numbers

Introduction:

➲ Show students the problem on slide 29, explaining how the jewels are evenly divided among the three archeologists on slide 30
➲ Move to slide 32, showing the same scenario with a numerator of 23 and explain how remainders work

Guided Practice:

➲ Students will be given a division worksheet and will employ the grouping method shown on the slideshow to solve problems
➲ After sufficient practice, the long division method will be implemented

Independent Work:

➲ Students will practice division in small groups, initially using the method shown on slide 33, and eventually using long division

Fractions

Learning Objectives:

- Students will learn about numerators and denominators, and what each represents in a fraction

Introduction:

- Show students the problem on slide 39, and ask students to draw how they believe the pizza should be shared equally among eight people
- Explain how each person gets one of those eighth

Guided Practice:

- Students will be given a fractions worksheet and will employ methods similar to those shown on the slideshow

Independent Work:

- Students will work on the fractions worksheet to strengthen their ability to identify and discern varying fractional amounts

DECIMALS

Learning Objectives:

- Students will learn about the tenths, hundredths, and thousandths places, and how to apply addition, subtraction, multiplication, and division to numbers with decimals

Introduction:

- Show students picture on slide 39, describing how decimals are part of a whole
- Continue on to slide 40, describing notation of decimals

Guided Practice:

- Work through the problem on slide 41 to illustrate that decimals undergo the same operations as whole numbers

Independent Work:

- Students will work on addition, subtraction, multiplication, and division worksheets to build confidence that employing previously taught methods is a viable strategy

PERCENTAGES

Learning Objectives:

- ⮑ Students will learn about percentages

Introduction:

- ⮑ Work through problem on slide 53
- ⮑ Use graphics on slide 57 to help students visualize what percentages are, and relate percentages to decimals by showing slide 56

Guided Practice:

- ⮑ Students will work through practice problems, using division and multiplication as shown on 54, 55, and 56

Independent Work:

- ⮑ Students will work through problems in small groups, solving equations from the worksheet

PROFIT/LOSS

Learning Objectives:

➲ Students will learn to determine whether different transactions result in a profit (net gain) or loss (net loss)

Introduction:

➲ Work through the problems on slides 45 and 48, showing students how to determine if the result is a profit (net gain) or loss (net loss)

Guided Practice:

➲ Students will work through practice problems, using subtraction to determine the answer, determining whether a net profit or net loss was the end result

Independent Work:

➲ Students will work through a worksheet of profit/loss problems using previously previously stated methods

UNITS OF MEASUREMENT

Learning Objectives:

➲ Students will learn about measurements of weight, time, temperature, and distance

Introduction:

➲ Students will observe slides 59 through 63, observing notation

Guided Practice:

➲ Students will be given a worksheet that further elaborates on previously seen measurements

Independent Work:

➲ Students will work through problems in small group, solving equations from the worksheet

ALGEBRA

Learning Objectives:

⮑ Students will learn basic algebra

Introduction:

⮑ Students will observe the problem on slide 65 to gain an understand of basic algebra

Guided Practice:

⮑ Symbols such as a box or a question mark can be used initially in problems so that students can more easily understand the concept of a missing or unknown value
⮑ Eventually, students should replace this sign with an "x". This will set them up for more advanced

Independent Work:

⮑ Students will work through problems in small group, solving equations from the worksheet

GEOMETRY

Learning Objectives:

➲ Students will learn about geometry, and how different shapes are defined

Introduction:

➲ Students will observe slides 69-74, identifying different shapes based on their features

Guided Practice:

➲ Students will be shown a variety of different shapes (drawn by the teacher) and will write down their answers on a piece of paper. After a few shapes have been shown, the teacher will reveal the answers and explaining how we understand which section each shape fits into

Independent Work:

➲ This will be a group exercise so no independent work will be present

GRAPHING

Learning Objectives:

- ⮑ Students will learn about graphing linear equations

Introduction:

- ⮑ The equation y = mx+b will be explained, using slides 77-80 to show how linear equations are graphed

Guided Practice:

- ⮑ The teacher may draw a graph, and using either a line or an equation, ask students to determine the other half

Independent Work:

- ⮑ Students will work through problems in small group, solving equations from the worksheet

Addition

—

What is addition?

- Addition is the process of making two groups of things into one group, also known as combining them
- Example: If Bobby has two toy cars and Johnny gives him one toy car, how many cars does he have?

Answer

- Three cars!

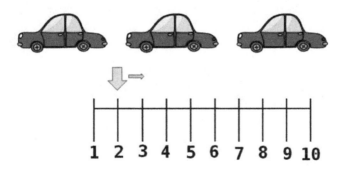

Addition with Larger Numbers

- What happens if we do an addition problem with larger numbers?
- Example: Millie brings 9 balls to the tennis court to hit with her friend, Sarah. Sarah brings 6 balls to the tennis court because she didn't know Millie was going to bring balls. How many tennis balls do they have total?

Answer

- 15 tennis balls!

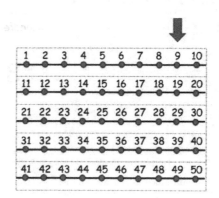

Column Addition

Hundreds	Tens	Ones

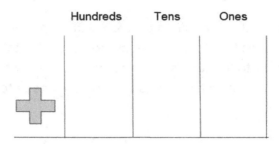

Column Addition

Hundreds	Tens	Ones
3	2	1
	2	4

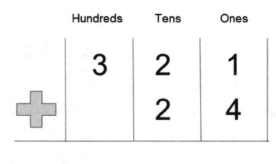

?

Answer

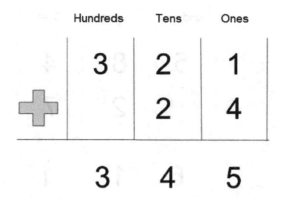

	Hundreds	Tens	Ones
	3	2	1
+		2	4
	3	4	5

Overflow

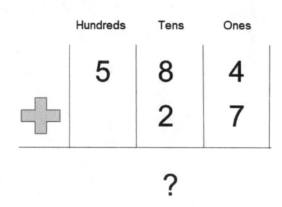

	Hundreds	Tens	Ones
	5	8	4
+		2	7
		?	

Answer

	Hundreds	Tens	Ones
	5	8	4
+		2	7
	6	1	1

Subtraction

—

What is Subtraction?

- Subtraction is the process of removing one or more things from a group
- Example: If Jake has four pieces of candy, and he decides to eat two of them, how many does he have left?

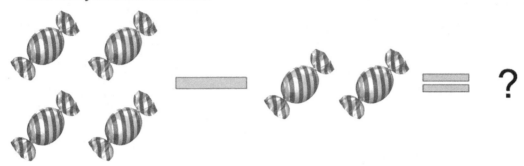

Answer

- Two pieces of candy!

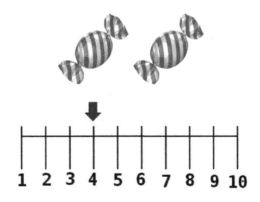

Subtraction with Larger Numbers

- Jeremy has 30 marbles in a bag. He decides to take out 20 to play with. How many of his marbles are still in the bag?

Stack Subtraction

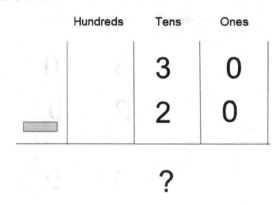

Hundreds	Tens	Ones
	3	0
	2	0
	?	

Stack Subtraction

	Hundreds	Tens	Ones
		3	0
		2	0
▬			

?

Answer

	Hundreds	Tens	Ones
		3	0
		2	0
▬			

1   0

Answer

- Ten marbles!

Multiplication

—

What is Multiplication?

- Multiplication is repeated addition
- When multiplying one number by another, the other number tells you how many times you will add
- For example: Timmy has five dollars in his piggy pank. After working at his job, he triples this amount. How much money does Timmy have now?

    3 ?

Multiplication

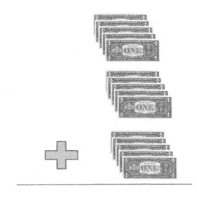

?

Multiplication

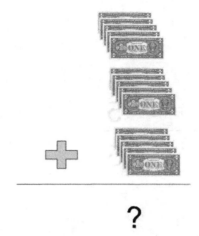

?

Multiplication

5
5
✚ 5
_____
?

Answer

$$
\begin{array}{r}
5 \\
5 \\
+\ 5 \\
\hline
15
\end{array}
$$

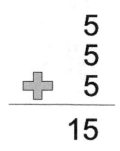

Answer

- Fifteen Dollars!

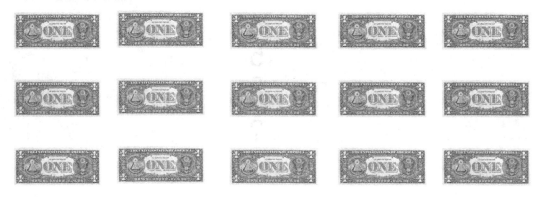

Stack Multiplication

- Just like addition and subtraction, we can use stack multiplication to multiply large numbers!

$$
\begin{array}{r}
3 \\
\times\ 3 \\
\hline
?
\end{array}
$$

Answer

$$
\begin{array}{r}
3 \\
\times\ 3 \\
\hline
9
\end{array}
$$

Division

What is Division?

- Division is when you separate a larger group into smaller groups
- When we divide, we typically choose a specific number to divide by, and make the larger number into smaller group. This number tells us how many individual numbers should be in each group.

What is Division?

- We use division every day when we share with others evenly
- Example: A group of 3 archeologists finds 21 jewels on an expedition. They want to share them equally. How many jewels should each archeologist get?

What is Division?

Answer

$$21 \div 3 = 7$$

Division with Remainders

- What happens if we do the same problem but we change the numbers slightly?
- New Example: A group of 3 archeologists finds 23 jewels on an expedition. They want to share them equally. How many jewels should each archeologist get?

Division with Remainders

Division of Remainders

Division with Remainders

23 ÷ 3 = 7 R 2

35

Long Division

$$9 \overline{)18}$$

Long Division

$$9 \overline{)\underline{18}}$$
$$18$$

with quotient 2

Fractions

———

What are Fractions?

- Fractions represent a part of a whole, and always have a top (numerator) and a bottom (denominator)
- You can think of fractions as a portion of a pizza

Numerator

Denominator

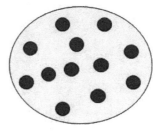

What are Fractions?

- Dillon wants to divide a pizza equally for him and his seven friends to share. What fraction of the pizza should each person get?

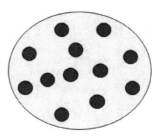

What are Fractions

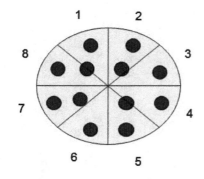

Number of People = 8

Total = 8

What are Fractions

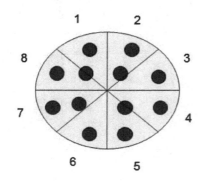

Each person should get
$\frac{1}{8}$ of the pizza

Decimals

What are Decimals?

- Similar to the remainders in divisions, decimals are used to express a part of a whole

1/10	1/10	1/10	1/10	1/10	1/10	1/10	1/10	1/10	1/10

What are Decimals?

- Decimals are shown with a dot after the number
- Each place behind the dot is one tenths place larger

■ _____ _____ _____

One tenth   One hundredth   One thousandth

Decimals in Currency

- Decimals are seen most prominently in currency
- Example: Jack goes to buy a gallon of milk from the store. The gallon of milk costs $3.99 Jack brought 4 dollars with him. What is his change?

$$\begin{array}{r} 4.00 \\ -\ 3.99 \\ \hline ? \end{array}$$

Decimals in Currency

$$\begin{array}{r} 4.00 \\ -\ 3.99 \\ \hline ? \end{array}$$

43

Decimals in Currency

- Decimals are seen most prominently in currency
- Example: Jack goes to buy a gallon of milk from the store. The gallon of milk costs $3.99 Jack brought 4 dollars with him. What is his change?

$$
\begin{array}{r}
4.00 \\
-\ 3.99 \\
\hline
.01
\end{array}
$$

Percentages

———

What are Percentages?

- Just like decimals, percentages tell us how much of a whole a specific part is
- Instead of using a period to show percentages, we use the percentage sign (%)
- Percentages are always out of 100, so 50% is really 50/100 or .5

What are Percentages?

- Joseph and Stan play on their soccer team together. Stan scores forty goals and Joseph scores sixty goals. What percent of the total goals have each scored?

What are Percentages?

Stan

$$\frac{40}{100} = .4 \times 100 = 40\%$$

What are Percentages?

- First get the total number of things
- Then divide your part by the whole

Stan

$$\frac{40}{100}$$

Joseph

$$\frac{60}{100}$$

What are Percentages?

Joseph

$$\frac{60}{100} = .6 \times 100 = 60\%$$

Answer

● Joseph scored 60% of the goals while Stan scored 40% of the goals

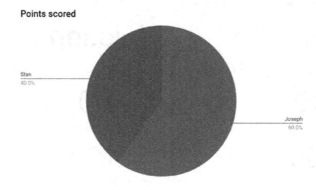

Points scored

Stan
40.0%

Joseph
60.0%

Profit/Loss

—

What is Profit/Loss?

- Profit/Loss questions are used to tell us how much money we've gained or lost
- Example: Bobby sells three pencils to Jack. Bobby bought the pencils for 50 cents and sold them to jack at 80 cents. Did Bobby make a profit?

What is Profit/Loss?

$$\begin{array}{r} 80 \\ -\ 50 \\ \hline ? \end{array}$$

What is Profit/Loss?

$$
\begin{array}{r}
80 \\
-50 \\
\hline
30
\end{array}
$$

What if...

- Bobby had a sale and his pencils are half off. Jack comes back to buy three more pencils, which cost 40 cents. It still costs Bobby 50 cents to buy the pencils. Did Bobby make a profit?

What if...

$$40 - 40 = \ ?$$

$$0 - 10 = \ ?$$

What if...

$$40 - 40 = 0$$

$$0 - 10 = -10$$

Units of Measurement

What are Units of Measurement?

- Units of measurement help us quantify how much of something there is
- The unit of measurement can also be changed by prefixes
- For example: 1000 grams = 1 kilogram

Milli-	One thousandth of (1/1000)
Centi-	One hundredth of (1/100)
Deci-	One tenth of (1/10)
Deca-	Ten of (x10)
Hecto-	One hundred of (x100)
Kilo-	One thousand of (x1000)

Weight

- Weight is in grams, and can be affected by the prefixes that we just discussed
- Weight is commonly talked about in grams or kilograms

Time

● Time is in seconds, but also has other units that don't have prefixes

60 Seconds	1 Minute
60 Minutes	1 Hour
24 Hours	1 Day
365 Days	1 Year

Temperature

● Temperature is usually in Celsius, sometimes in Fahrenheit
● The freezing point on the Celsius scale is 0 degrees, while the boiling point is 100 degrees

Distance

- Distance is in terms of meters

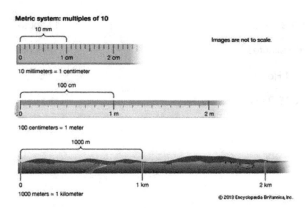

Metric system: multiples of 10

10 mm

Images are not to scale.

0   1 cm   2 cm

10 millimeters = 1 centimeter

100 cm

0   1 m   2 m

100 centimeters = 1 meter

1000 m

0   1 km   2 km

1000 meters = 1 kilometer

© 2013 Encyclopædia Britannica, Inc.

Algebra

What is Algebra?

- Algebra is when we use letters as placeholders in an equation for unknown numbers
- Letters like x and y are commonly used for this
- For example: x + 2 = 4

What is Algebra?

- X + 2 = 4

    - 2 - 2

- X = 2

What is Algebra?

- X - 3 = 6

    + 3 + 3

- X = 9

Geometry

Circle

- A circle is a shape that is round and has the same distance from the center to the edge all around it

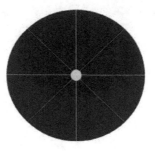

Triangle

- A triangle is a three sided figure
- The length of the two smaller sides must be greater than the larger side

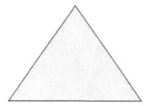

Square

- A square is a four sided figure
- Each side is the same length

Rectangle

- Like a square, a rectangle is a four sided figure, however the length of the sides are not the same
- Only two pairs of sides are equal

Rhombus

- Just like a square the length of a rhombus' sides are all equal
- The difference between a square and a rhombus is the angles. Parallel angles are equal, but not all four angles are equal

Trapezoid

- A trapezoid is a four sided figure that has one set of parallel sides

Graphing

What is Graphing?

Y=mx+b

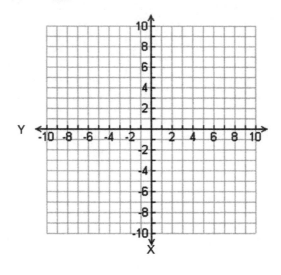

What is Graphing?

- Graph y = x + 5

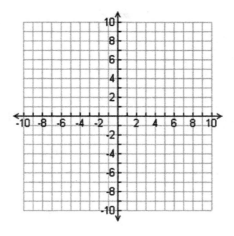

What is Graphing?

● Graph y = x + 5

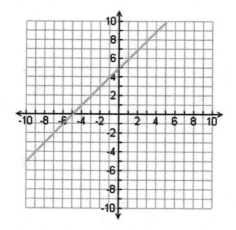

What is Graphing?

● Graph y = 2x

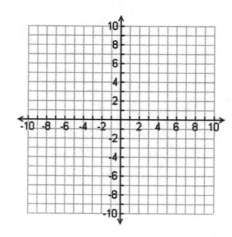

What is Graphing?

- Graph y = 2x

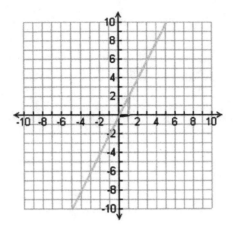

ADDITION

So, what is addition? Slide two says that addition is the process of combining two groups of things into one group, but what does that mean? It might sound complicated, but addition is actually something that we do everyday. For example, when you buy items at a store, the prices of each item are combined or "added" together to give the total price you pay. (Ask students what they buy). So let's take a look at our first example. It says that Bobby has two cars and Johnny has one car. Johnny decides to give his car to Bobby. How many cars does Bobby have now? Let's use our definition of addition to help us solve this. We know that addition is when you combine two different groups of things to make a single group that is even larger. So let's take the two groups and make it one, and then let's count how many there are total. Since we added Johnny's one car to Bobby's group of two cars, we've made the number of cars Bobby has bigger and can count the new number of cars he has. (Count the cars with the students). As we can see here, the new total is three, so two plus one equals three.

Let's try doing addition with some larger numbers. Here we have a problem that says Millie brings 9 balls to the tennis court to hit with her friend, Sarah. Sarah brings 6 balls to the tennis court because she didn't know Millie was going to bring balls. How many tennis balls do they have total?

In this problem we're adding together nine and six, so we're clearly going to go into the double digits. But how do we do that for this problem? As you can see it isn't much different from our first example. (Draw one group of six balls and another group of nine balls on the board or use slide 4) We count up the total number of tennis balls to get our new total, 15. We can write this problem out as 9 plus 6 equals 15. To get this we would take nine, and count up by six numbers. (Point to depiction on the board or slideshow) By doing that, we're combining the two numbers, therefore we're doing addition.

Let's try even bigger numbers. For this, we're going to use a method called column addition to break it down. It helps us add together two-digit numbers by using one digit addition. We add the ones places of the two numbers together, then the tens places, then the hundreds places, and so on. The most important thing is that we start on the right, in the ones place. Let's try 321 + 24. First, we have to line up the numbers. Then, we start on the right with our ones place. (Instructor covers everything but the ones place with hand) We see 1+4. So we count four up from one, and we get five (Use fingers to show this). So we write 5 below the line, and move on to the tens place. (Cover up the ones place) In the tens place we have 2+2, So we go two up from 2 to get 4. Then we write 4 below the line and continue to the hundreds place. Here we have 3 in 321 but our other number, 24, doesn't have anything in the hundreds place. Since there isn't anything to add to it, we can keep it as 3 and just move it down to the bottom. Now we have a new number, 345, which is our total for 321 + 24. When doing stack addition, if a column (stack) is greater than or equal to ten, it must overflow into the next column. This means that the value of the number that was previously in that column has moved up by one ten's place.

SUBTRACTION

Let's take a look at subtraction. Subtraction is the opposite of addition, so instead of combining two groups, we're separating one group from another. In other words, instead of making a number bigger as in addition, we're making it smaller. Let's take a look at our example. If Jake has four pieces of candy, and he decides to eat two of them, how many does he have left? (Draw four pieces of candy on the board and cross out two of them). To find out how many pieces he'll have left, we're going to want to count down from four by two. We end up with two pieces of candy, which is the new total after subtracting the two that Jake ate.

Let's try doing subtraction with larger numbers now. It says that Jeremy has 30 marbles in a bag. He decides to take out 18 to play with. How many of his marbles are still in the bag? How do you think we need to write this equation to solve this problem? (Should end up with $30 - 18 = ?$) For a problem like this that has larger numbers, let's use the stack method that we used for addition, but use subtraction instead. As you can see, the way the columns are set up is the same. The only thing that has changed is the sign that's in front of the problem. This minus sign, instead of a plus sign, tells us that we're going to be doing subtraction instead of addition. Like we did with addition, we focus on one column at a time. Let's try 30-20. Look at the first column. If we break it down, it says zero minus zero. The answer to that is zero because we aren't actually subtracting anything there. We can move onto the tens place, and there we have 3 - 2, and we count down by one to get 2. So we find that 30-20=10.

MULTIPLICATION

Now let's try multiplication. Multiplication may sound complicated, but we've already done it. Multiplication is really just repeated addition. The number on the left is the number that we'll be adding repeatedly, and the number on the right tells us how many times we'll be adding it. Let's take a look at our example problem. Here it says that Timmy has five dollars in his piggy pank. After working at his job, he has 3 times this amount. How much money does Timmy have now? So, in this problem, Timmy's five dollars is multiplied by three. We write this out as 5 x 3, or 5 + 5 + 5. So we can solve it like our previous addition problems. 5+5=10 and 10+5=15.

Now let's do the same problem, but just replace the sign that's in front of it. The x for multiplication may look intimidating, but just remember that it's the same thing as adding a number to itself!

DIVISION

So what is division? Division is when you take a group of things and separate, or divide, it into smaller groups. It's the exact opposite of multiplication. The number of things in those smaller groups is determined by the number you divide by. This is a little more complicated than the previous topics, so let's take a look at a practice problem. The problem says that a group of 3 archeologists finds 21 jewels on an expedition. They want to share them equally. How many jewels should each archeologist get? For this we're going to want to first try to evenly divide up the jewels, and to do that we're going to mark them with different colors. Now we're going to count up the totals for each of the three colors. We can see that each totals seven, so that means 21 divided by three is seven. But what happens if the numbers don't add up to the same number? Let's try to change the numbers around for that problem, and see what happens. If we try that with 23 jewels, we see that we have eight blue and red jewels, while we only have seven purple jewels. The answer can't be eight, since we aren't able to give each person in the group eight jewels, so it has to be seven since each group has at least seven. But what happens with the two jewels that we can't give to anyone? They become the remainder, or what's left over. To show this, we add an R and the number of jewels left over to the end of our answer. So, in this case, we have 7 R2. Let's try doing this with larger numbers. To do so, we'll be doing what's called long division, which, as the name implies, allows us to do division with larger numbers. Let's try 18 divided by nine. To find out how many times nine goes into 18, we'll try to estimate it first. If we multiply nine by two, it becomes eighteen. Since this goes into 18 exactly, that's our answer.

FRACTIONS

What are fractions? Fractions are what we use to describe a portion of something. A fraction is described as a part over a whole. As we can see on this slide (slide 39), there are two parts to a fraction: a numerator (the part) and a denominator (the whole). We'll be using a pizza to show how fractions work. Let's take a look at our first problem. Dillon wants to divide a pizza equally for him and his seven friends to share. What portion of the pizza does each person get? To determine this, we're going to first want to find out how many people will share the pizza. We can see that there are eight people total. This total will be our "whole", so it will be our denominator. Now we need to figure out what our numerator would be. To do this, we need to remember what we're trying to do. We're trying to figure out what portion of the pie each person gets. Since there are eight people, and we've determined that the denominator is eight, we know that each person should get one eighth. This assures that the pizza is shared evenly among everyone. That's how we find out that the numerator should be one, because each person will get one eighth.

DECIMALS

Like fractions, we use decimals to describe however many parts there are of a whole. Decimals are marked by a period, and to the right of it is one tenth smaller. A common decimal is .5. This means five out of ten, which would be one half. Decimals are only a part of a whole, but we can still do addition, subtraction, multiplication, and even division with them. Let's take a look at an example. Jack goes to buy a gallon of milk from the store. The gallon of milk costs $3.99 Jack brought 4 dollars with him. What is his change? To do this problem, we're going to need to use the column method of subtraction. So we'll borrow a one and move it to the tenths place. Now that the tenths place is 10 - 9, we can see that the hundredths place is 0 - 9, which doesn't work, so we'll need to borrow once more. Now each place can be subtracted properly, and we can see that our answer is 0.01 when we bring the decimal down, otherwise known as 1 cent.

PERCENTAGES

What are Percentages? Percentages are like decimals, because they tell us what part of a whole something is. Percentages are always out of one hundred, and to find the percent of something, you must think about what part of the group it takes up. Let's try a practice problem. Joseph and Stan play on their soccer team together. Joseph scores sixty goals and Stan scores forty goals. What percent of the total goals have each scored? To find the percentage each scored, we first need the total goals, which is one hundred, because forty plus sixty is one hundred. Then to find what percent each scored, we put the part over the whole. So for Joseph, that would be sixty over one hundred, which equals .6. To get from .6 to a percent, we're going to multiply the decimal by 100. This gets us 60, which is really 60 percent. For Stan, it would be forty over one hundred, which would equal .4, or forty percent.

PROFIT/LOSS

So what's profit/loss? In a math situation concerning money, profit is when you've made money and loss is when you've lost money. This is something that store owners do every day to see if the products that they're selling are profitable. Let's look at our practice problem. Bobby sells three pencils to Jack. Bobby bought the pencils for 50 cents each and sold them to jack at 80 cents each. Did Bobby make a profit when he sold the pencils or did he lose money? To find out, we have to subtract the amount of money he paid for the pencils from the amount of money he sold the pencils for. We can write this equation as 3 x 80 cents minus 3 x 50 cents. From there, we get positive 90 cents. Since the number is positive, we know that Bobby profited by thirty cents per pencil. But what happens if the money that Bobby paid for the pencils is less than the amount he sells them for? In other words, what if the original price is greater than the selling price? Imagine that Bobby had a sale and his pencils are half off. So instead of costing 80 cents, each pencil now costs half of that, or 40 cents. Jack buys three pencils, now paying 3 x 40 cents, which equals $1.20. But Bobby paid $1.50 = 3 x 50 cent's to get the pencils. Did Bobby make a profit? Since he paid more for the pencils than he received from Jack, we know that Bobby did not make a profit, and instead had a loss of $1.50-$1.20 = 30 cents. Bobby lost ten cents per pencil.

Units of Measurement

What are units of measurement? (Ask the children if they know any units of measurement) Units of measurement tell us how much of something there is. These units can also be more specific, and can be changed by prefixes to tell us how large or small a unit is. Let's take a look at one unit that is really important: weight. Weight is in grams, and tells us how heavy something is. To tells us more specifically what magnitude of weight it is, we can use prefixes. The prefixes are milli-, centi-, deci-, deca-, hecto-, kilo-. Milli-, centi-, and deci- mean one thousandth, one hundredth, and one tenth respectively. Deca-, hecto-, kilo- are ten times, one hundred times, and one thousand times. Let's move on to time. Time is calculated in seconds. A second is about the amount of time it takes for you to say "One mississippi". Sixty of these seconds come together to make a minute. If you take sixty of those minutes and put them together, you form an hour. If you go even further, and take twenty four of these hours, you get a day. Three hundred and sixty five of these days are a year. What about temperature? Temperature is in Celsius, and the freezing point is at zero degrees, and the boiling point is at 100 degrees. The freezing point and boiling point are where water freezes and boils. Depending on how close the number is to zero or one hundred, that tells us if it's hot or cold. There's one more important unit, which is distance. Distance tells us how far something is. Distance has the same prefixes as weight, but the unit is different. For distance, we use meters. A meter is about three feet, and the varying distances can be shown by this picture: centimeters are very small, while kilometers are very large.

ALGEBRA

Let's look at algebra. Algebra is something that looks very scary, but it isn't hard once you get the hang of it. Algebra is essentially when you solve for a missing number. To do so, we put a letter in the place of the missing number. Letters like x, y, and z are commonly used here. Let's dive into a problem, because once we get started it won't be that difficult. The problem is x plus two equals four. To solve this problem, all we have to do is get X alone. To do this, we're going to subtract two from both sides, and we get X alone. The problem now says X = 2. If we do a similar problem, but with subtraction, the opposite happens. Our next problem says X minus three equals six. To solve this, we're going to add three to both sides, and we get that X equals nine.

GEOMETRY

What is geometry? Geometry is math that focuses on shapes. We'll be taking a look at different shapes to get an idea of how to determine and define what they are. A circle is a round shape, and the distance from the center to any point on the edge is the same. If you take a look at the picture, you can see the lines that go from the center to the edge. Since this is a circle, we know that the length of them is equal. What are triangles? Triangles are three sided figures. Triangles that all have equal sides like this one are called equilateral triangles. Triangles that are equal on two sides are called isosceles triangles. A triangle that isn't equal on any of its sides is called a scalene triangle. Squares are four sided figures that are equal on all sides. A four sided figure that isn't equal on all four sides is called a rectangle. Instead, a rectangle has two pairs of sides that are equal. A rhombus is a four sided figure that has equal sides like a square, but has angles that are different. A trapezoid is a four sided figure that has one set of parallel sides.

GRAPHING

Let's take a look at graphing. Graphing is what we do to plot or map out something. Graphs have to dimensions, up and down, which is called the y - dimension, and left and right, which is called the x dimension. We use the formula Y = mx+b to define a line, and see where it goes. Let's explain the variables before we do anything with them. The x and the y are going to be our coordinates, and we'll use them to find our specific location. The m is our slope. The slope tells us how much we're going up by, and in what direction we're traveling. The b is our y intercept. This tells us where we're touching the line x = 0.

Solve the Equations

1) $z + 6 = -11$

2) $36 = -3c$

3) $-12 = -7 + d$

4) $6 = n - 5$

5) $-20 = -5h$

6) $\frac{x}{3} = -9$

7) $-12 = -7 + k$

8) $-2v = 10$

9) $7r = -42$

10) $5 = \frac{f}{5}$

Professor Zach's Basic Algebra Practice

Solve the Equations

1) $z + 6 = -11$

$z = -17$

2) $36 = -3c$

$c = -12$

3) $-12 = -7 + d$

$d = -5$

4) $6 = n - 5$

$n = 11$

5) $-20 = -5h$

$h = 4$

6) $\frac{x}{3} = -9$

$x = -27$

7) $-12 = -7 + k$

$k = -5$

8) $-2v = 10$

$v = -5$

9) $7r = -42$

$r = -6$

10) $5 = \frac{f}{5}$

$f = 25$

Professor Zach's Basic Algebra Practice

Converting Between Percents, Decimals, and Fractions

Convert Decimal to Percent

0.298 =	0.793 =	0.74 =
1.95 =	0.789 =	1.59 =
1.73 =	0.325 =	1.53 =
0.08 =	1.16 =	0.26 =
0.57 =	1.67 =	1.58 =

Convert Decimal to Fraction

0.07 =	0.873 =	0.855 =
1.24 =	0.192 =	1.48 =
0.464 =	1.7 =	1.66 =
1.27 =	1.34 =	0.195 =
0.268 =	1.8 =	0.844 =

Professor Zach's Decimal Conversion Practice

Converting Between Percents, Decimals, and Fractions

Convert Decimal to Percent

0.298 = 29.8 %	0.793 = 79.3 %	0.74 = 74 %
1.95 = 195 %	0.789 = 78.9 %	1.59 = 159 %
1.73 = 173 %	0.325 = 32.5 %	1.53 = 153 %
0.08 = 8 %	1.16 = 116 %	0.26 = 26 %
0.57 = 57 %	1.67 = 167 %	1.58 = 158 %

Convert Decimal to Fraction

$0.07 = \frac{7}{100}$

$1.24 = \frac{124}{100} = \frac{31}{25}$

$0.464 = \frac{464}{1000} = \frac{58}{125}$

$1.27 = \frac{127}{100}$

$0.268 = \frac{268}{1000} = \frac{67}{250}$

$0.873 = \frac{873}{1000}$

$0.192 = \frac{192}{1000} = \frac{24}{125}$

$1.7 = \frac{17}{10}$

$1.34 = \frac{134}{100} = \frac{67}{50}$

$1.8 = \frac{18}{10} = \frac{9}{5}$

$0.855 = \frac{855}{1000} = \frac{171}{200}$

$1.48 = \frac{148}{100} = \frac{37}{25}$

$1.66 = \frac{166}{100} = \frac{83}{50}$

$0.195 = \frac{195}{1000} = \frac{39}{200}$

$0.844 = \frac{844}{1000} = \frac{211}{250}$

Professor Zach's Decimal Conversion Practice

10	35	4	13	50
+ 83	+ 53	+ 89	+ 38	+ 93

25	12	29	26	83
+ 56	+ 97	+ 24	+ 1	+ 69

91	28	93	74	62
+ 52	+ 81	+ 46	+ 99	+ 9

Professor Zach's Double Digit Addition Practice

```
   10        35         4        13        50
 + 83      + 53      + 89      + 38      + 93
 ----      ----      ----      ----      ----
   93        88        93        51       143


   25        12        29        26        83
 + 56      + 97      + 24      +  1      + 69
 ----      ----      ----      ----      ----
   81       109        53        27       152


   91        28        93        74        62
 + 52      + 81      + 46      + 99      +  9
 ----      ----      ----      ----      ----
  143       109       139       173        71
```

Professor Zach's Double Digit Addition Practice

| 91.42 | 83.22 | 30.85 | 98.17 | 44.14 |
| - 82.55 | - 12.39 | - 25.77 | - 17.38 | - 32.99 |

| 80.25 | 93.67 | 85.54 | 79.18 | 68.66 |
| - 17.13 | - 60.36 | - 44.27 | - 30.33 | - 13.39 |

| 75.67 | 36.18 | 57.19 | 91.53 | 88.54 |
| - 21.23 | - 17.71 | - 35.69 | - 54.29 | - 54.13 |

Professor Zach's Double Digit Decimal Subtraction Practice

91.42	83.22	30.85	98.17	44.14
- 82.55	- 12.39	- 25.77	- 17.38	- 32.99
8.87	70.83	5.08	80.79	11.15

80.25	93.67	85.54	79.18	68.66
- 17.13	- 60.36	- 44.27	- 30.33	- 13.39
63.12	33.31	41.27	48.85	55.27

75.67	36.18	57.19	91.53	88.54
- 21.23	- 17.71	- 35.69	- 54.29	- 54.13
54.44	18.47	21.50	37.24	34.41

Professor Zach's Double Digit Decimal Subtraction Practice

88	68	85	41	20
x 22	x 33	x 78	x 57	x 17

77	46	88	40	12
x 85	x 38	x 88	x 22	x 39

96	83	69	22	71
x 69	x 27	x 18	x 94	x 16

Professor Zach's Double Digit Multiplication Practice

88	68	85	41	20
x 22	x 33	x 78	x 57	x 17
1936	2244	6630	2337	340

77	46	88	40	12
x 85	x 38	x 88	x 22	x 39
6545	1748	7744	880	468

96	83	69	22	71
x 69	x 27	x 18	x 94	x 16
6624	2241	1242	2068	1136

Professor Zach's Double Digit Multiplication Practice

86	96	62	18	32
- 1	- 12	- 11	- 6	- 8

50	61	98	35	83
- 0	- 51	- 56	- 13	- 58

52	85	86	99	55
- 18	- 43	- 42	- 73	- 45

Professor Zach's Double Digit Subtraction Practice

86	96	62	18	32
- 1	- 12	- 11	- 6	- 8
85	84	51	12	24

50	61	98	35	83
- 0	- 51	- 56	- 13	- 58
50	10	42	22	25

52	85	86	99	55
- 18	- 43	- 42	- 73	- 45
34	42	44	26	10

Professor Zach's Double Digit Subtraction Practice

Converting Between Percents, Decimals, and Fractions

Convert Fraction to Decimal

$\frac{7}{16}$ = $\frac{5}{8}$ = $\frac{7}{10}$ =

$\frac{1}{50}$ = $\frac{3}{8}$ = $\frac{11}{16}$ =

$\frac{5}{8}$ = $\frac{44}{25}$ = $\frac{39}{40}$ =

$\frac{3}{8}$ = $\frac{16}{10}$ = $\frac{3}{16}$ =

$\frac{16}{50}$ = $\frac{3}{8}$ = $\frac{8}{25}$ =

Convert Fraction to Percent

$\frac{7}{8}$ = $\frac{19}{50}$ = $\frac{46}{25}$ =

$\frac{9}{20}$ = $\frac{3}{8}$ = $\frac{29}{20}$ =

$\frac{22}{20}$ = $\frac{17}{20}$ = $\frac{9}{20}$ =

$\frac{19}{10}$ = $\frac{7}{10}$ = $\frac{13}{16}$ =

$\frac{3}{8}$ = $\frac{88}{50}$ = $\frac{21}{25}$ =

Professor Zach's Fraction Conversion Practice

Converting Between Percents, Decimals, and Fractions

Convert Fraction to Decimal

$\frac{7}{16}$ = 0.4375 $\frac{5}{8}$ = 0.625 $\frac{7}{10}$ = 0.7

$\frac{1}{50}$ = 0.02 $\frac{3}{8}$ = 0.375 $\frac{11}{16}$ = 0.6875

$\frac{5}{8}$ = 0.625 $\frac{44}{25}$ = 1.76 $\frac{39}{40}$ = 0.975

$\frac{3}{8}$ = 0.375 $\frac{16}{10}$ = 1.6 $\frac{3}{16}$ = 0.1875

$\frac{16}{50}$ = 0.32 $\frac{3}{8}$ = 0.375 $\frac{8}{25}$ = 0.32

Convert Fraction to Percent

$\frac{7}{8}$ = 87.5 % $\frac{19}{50}$ = 38 % $\frac{46}{25}$ = 184 %

$\frac{9}{20}$ = 45 % $\frac{3}{8}$ = 37.5 % $\frac{29}{20}$ = 145 %

$\frac{22}{20}$ = 110 % $\frac{17}{20}$ = 85 % $\frac{9}{20}$ = 45 %

$\frac{19}{10}$ = 190 % $\frac{7}{10}$ = 70 % $\frac{13}{16}$ = 81.25 %

$\frac{3}{8}$ = 37.5 % $\frac{88}{50}$ = 176 % $\frac{21}{25}$ = 84 %

Professor Zach's Fraction Conversion Practice

Name : _____   Score : _____

Teacher : _____   Date : _____

What is the Fraction of the Shaded Area ?

1) _____

2) _____

3) _____

4) _____

5) _____

6) _____

7) _____

8) _____

9) _____

10) _____

Shade the Figure with the Indicated Fraction.

11) $\dfrac{8}{9}$

12) $\dfrac{4}{11}$

13) $\dfrac{7}{9}$

14) $\dfrac{4}{12}$

15) $\dfrac{8}{12}$

16) $\dfrac{4}{7}$

17) $\dfrac{1}{10}$

18) $\dfrac{6}{7}$

19) $\dfrac{3}{5}$

20) $\dfrac{4}{6}$

Professor Zach's Fraction Practice

Name : _____   Score : _____

Teacher : _____   Date : _____

What is the Fraction of the Shaded Area ?

1) $\dfrac{2}{8}$

2) $\dfrac{10}{11}$

3) $\dfrac{1}{4}$

4) $\dfrac{1}{7}$

5) $\dfrac{5}{12}$

6) $\dfrac{10}{12}$

7) $\dfrac{1}{9}$

8) $\dfrac{3}{8}$

9) $\dfrac{2}{11}$

10) $\dfrac{3}{6}$

Shade the Figure with the Indicated Fraction.

11) $\dfrac{8}{9}$

12) $\dfrac{4}{11}$

13) $\dfrac{7}{9}$

14) $\dfrac{4}{12}$

15) $\dfrac{8}{12}$

16) $\dfrac{4}{7}$

17) $\dfrac{1}{10}$

18) $\dfrac{6}{7}$

19) $\dfrac{3}{5}$

20) $\dfrac{4}{6}$

Professor Zach's Fraction Practice

97

Four Quadrant Graphing Puzzle

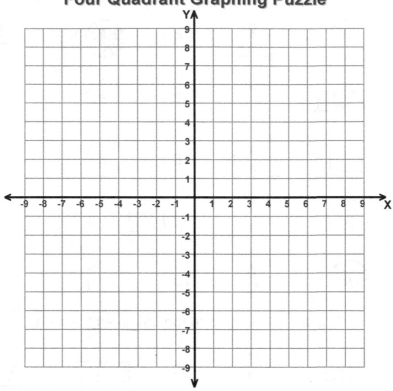

Connect each sequence of points with a line.

(-3,0) , (-4,-1) , (-6,-2) , (-6,-3) , (-5,-4) , (-4,-4) , (-3,-4) , (1,-2) End of Sequence

(-1,1) , (5,3) , (6,5) , (7,5) , (7,3) , (9,2) , (8,1.5) , (6,2) , (2,-.5) End of Sequence

(-5,-3) , (-5.5,0) , (-5,0) , (-5,-6) , (-4.5,-6) , (-5,-3) End of Sequence

(-9,3) , (-7,4) , (7,-3) , (5,-4) , (-9,3) End of Sequence

(-6,-2) , (-4,-3) , (-2,-2) , (-1,-1) End of Sequence

(5,3) , (4,4) , (4.5,4.5) , (5.5,4) End of Sequence

(-4,-1) , (-2,-2) End of Sequence

What is the shape ?   _____

Professor Zach's Graphing Practice

Four Quadrant Graphing Puzzle

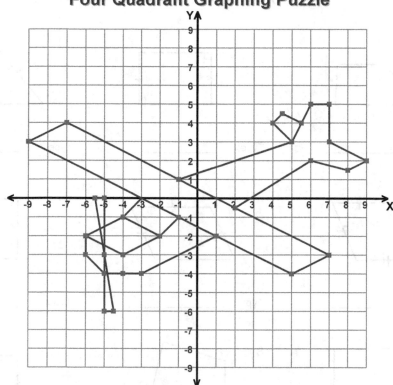

Connect each sequence of points with a line.

(-3,0) , (-4,-1) , (-6,-2) , (-6,-3) , (-5,-4) , (-4,-4) , (-3,-4) , (1,-2) End of Sequence

(-1,1) , (5,3) , (6,5) , (7,5) , (7,3) , (9,2) , (8,1.5) , (6,2) , (2,-.5) End of Sequence

(-5,-3) , (-5.5,0) , (-5,0) , (-5,-6) , (-4.5,-6) , (-5,-3) End of Sequence

(-9,3) , (-7,4) , (7,-3) , (5,-4) , (-9,3) End of Sequence

(-6,-2) , (-4,-3) , (-2,-2) , (-1,-1) End of Sequence

(5,3) , (4,4) , (4.5,4.5) , (5.5,4) End of Sequence

(-4,-1) , (-2,-2) End of Sequence

What is the shape ?   Airplane_____

Professor Zach's Graphing Practice

99

Identify the Type For Each Quadrilateral.

1)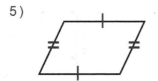

Type: _____

2)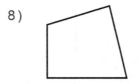

Type: _____

3)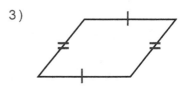

Type: _____

4)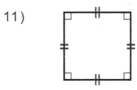

Type: _____

5)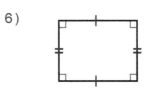

Type: _____

6)

Type: _____

7)

Type: _____

8)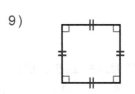

Type: _____

9)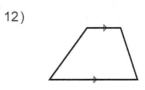

Type: _____

10)

Type: _____

11)

Type: _____

12)

Type: _____

Professor Zach's Identifying Quadrilaterals Practice

Name : _____   Score : _____

Teacher : _____   Date : _____

Identify the Type For Each Quadrilateral.

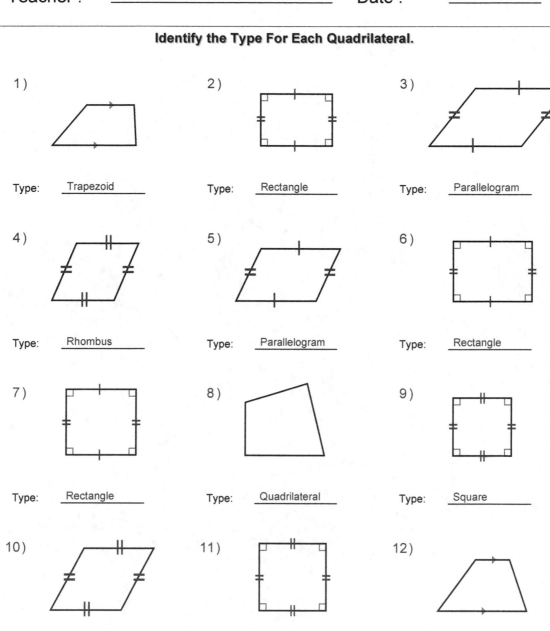

1)

Type: Trapezoid

2)

Type: Rectangle

3)

Type: Parallelogram

4)

Type: Rhombus

5)

Type: Parallelogram

6)

Type: Rectangle

7)

Type: Rectangle

8)

Type: Quadrilateral

9)

Type: Square

10)

Type: Rhombus

11)

Type: Square

12)

Type: Trapezoid

Professor Zach's Identifying Quadrilaterals Practice

Conversion Factors

General Conversion Factors

Length

To Obtain	Multiply	By
Feet	Miles	5280
Yards	Feet	1/3
Yards	Miles	1760
Feet	Yards	3
Miles	Feet	1.89394×10^{-4}
Miles	Yards	5.68182×10^{-4}

Weight

To Obtain	Multiply	By
Tons	Pounds	2000
Pounds	Tons	5.0×10^{-4}
Ounces	Pounds	16
Pounds	Ounces	0.0625

Area

To Obtain	Multiply	By
Square Feet	Acres	43560
Acres	Square Feet	2.2957×10^{-5}
Square Yards	Acres	4840
Acres	Square Yards	2.06612×10^{-4}

Speed

To Obtain	Multiply	By
Feet per Second	Miles per Hour	1.46667
Miles per Hour	Feet per Second	0.681818

Reading a Metric Ruler

How many Centimeters ?

62 63 64 65 66 67 68 69 70 71

_____

68 69 70 71 72 73 74 75 76 77

_____

82 83 84 85 86 87 88 89 90 91

_____

58 59 60 61 62 63 64 65 66 67

_____

37 38 39 40 41 42 43 44 45 46

_____

14 15 16 17 18 19 20 21 22 23

_____

43 44 45 46 47 48 49 50 51 52

_____

80 81 82 83 84 85 86 87 88 89

_____

Professor Zach's Metric Conversion Practice

Name : _____   Score : _____

Teacher : _____   Date : _____

Reading a Metric Ruler

How many Centimeters ?

70.65 cm
or
706.5 mm

74.55 cm
or
745.5 mm

82.45 cm
or
824.5 mm

60.2 cm
or
602 mm

38.85 cm
or
388.5 mm

13.6 cm
or
136 mm

49.8 cm
or
498 mm

81.55 cm
or
815.5 mm

Professor Zach's Metric Conversion Practice

Word Problems

1) Alyssa loves eating fruits. Alyssa paid $12.26 for apples, and $6.51 for grapes with a $20 bill. How much change did Alyssa receive?   _____

2) Sara went to the mall on Saturday to buy clothes. She paid $7.05 on a shirt and $11.10 on a jacket with a $20 bill. How much money did Sara get in change?   _____

3) Alyssa joined her school's band. She bought a flute for $87.58, and a song book which was $9.93 with a $100 bill. How much change was Alyssa given?   _____

4) Mary purchased a Superman game for $10.54, and a Spiderman game for $13.12 with two $20 bills. How much change did Mary get?   _____

5) Joan loves trading cards. She bought 4 packs of basketball cards for $5.64 each, and a deck of baseball cards for $8.21 with two $20 bills. How much change did Joan get?   _____

6) Alyssa got fast food for lunch. Alyssa paid $4.31 on a salad and $5.76 on soup with two $10 bills. What was the change from the purchase?   _____

7) Joan paid $4.03 on a gerbil toy, and a cage cost her $5.59 with a $20 bill. How much change did Joan receive?   _____

8) For his car, Fred paid $95.53 on speakers and $73.10 on new tires with two $100 bills. How much did Fred get in change?   _____

9) On Tuesday, Melanie paid $9.72 each on two tickets to a movie theater. She also borrowed a movie for $14.46. Melanie paid with two $20 bills. How much change did Melanie receive?   _____

10) Sandy bought some toys. She bought marbles for $8.61, and paid $5.73 on a football with a $20 bill. How much change from the purchase?   _____

Professor Zach's Money Word Problems Practice

Word Problems

1) Alyssa loves eating fruits. Alyssa paid $12.26 for apples, and $6.51 for grapes with a $20 bill. How much change did Alyssa receive?

$1.23 _____

2) Sara went to the mall on Saturday to buy clothes. She paid $7.05 on a shirt and $11.10 on a jacket with a $20 bill. How much money did Sara get in change?

$1.85 _____

3) Alyssa joined her school's band. She bought a flute for $87.58, and a song book which was $9.93 with a $100 bill. How much change was Alyssa given?

$2.49 _____

4) Mary purchased a Superman game for $10.54, and a Spiderman game for $13.12 with two $20 bills. How much change did Mary get?

$16.34 _____

5) Joan loves trading cards. She bought 4 packs of basketball cards for $5.64 each, and a deck of baseball cards for $8.21 with two $20 bills. How much change did Joan get?

$9.23 _____

6) Alyssa got fast food for lunch. Alyssa paid $4.31 on a salad and $5.76 on soup with two $10 bills. What was the change from the purchase?

$9.93 _____

7) Joan paid $4.03 on a gerbil toy, and a cage cost her $5.59 with a $20 bill. How much change did Joan receive?

$10.38 _____

8) For his car, Fred paid $95.53 on speakers and $73.10 on new tires with two $100 bills. How much did Fred get in change?

$31.37 _____

9) On Tuesday, Melanie paid $9.72 each on two tickets to a movie theater. She also borrowed a movie for $14.46. Melanie paid with two $20 bills. How much change did Melanie receive?

$6.10 _____

10) Sandy bought some toys. She bought marbles for $8.61, and paid $5.73 on a football with a $20 bill. How much change from the purchase?

$5.66 _____

Professor Zach's Money Word Problems Practice

Percentage Calculations

Round your answer to two decimal places.

1) 0.58 x 36 = ___

2) 77 ÷ 13 % = ___

3) 16 ÷ 24 % = ___

4) 35% x 91 = ___

5) 90 ÷ 0.91 = ___

6) 3% x 44 = ___

7) 0.9 x 95 = ___

8) 42 ÷ 43 = ___ %

9) 35 ÷ 63 = ___ %

10) 83 ÷ 0.87 = ___

Professor Zach's Percentage Calculation Practice

Percentage Calculations

Round your answer to two decimal places.

1) 0.58 x 36 = 20.88

6) 3% x 44 = 1.32

2) 77 ÷ 13 % = 592.31

7) 0.9 x 95 = 85.50

3) 16 ÷ 24 % = 66.67

8) 42 ÷ 43 = 97.67 %

4) 35% x 91 = 31.85

9) 35 ÷ 63 = 55.56 %

5) 90 ÷ 0.91 = 98.90

10) 83 ÷ 0.87 = 95.40

Professor Zach's Percentage Calculation Practice

Converting Between Percents, Decimals, and Fractions

Convert Percent to Decimal

63 % =	45.8 % =	139 % =
66 % =	43 % =	67.1 % =
131 % =	98.9 % =	81 % =
144 % =	64.3 % =	6 % =
24 % =	52.6 % =	17 % =

Convert Percent to Fraction

123 % =	49 % =	107 % =
47.1 % =	111 % =	132 % =
64.2 % =	17.4 % =	108 % =
63 % =	67 % =	194 % =
125 % =	52.5 % =	12.5 % =

Professor Zach's Percentage Conversion Practice

Converting Between Percents, Decimals, and Fractions

Convert Percent to Decimal

63 % = 0.63	45.8 % = 0.458	139 % = 1.39
66 % = 0.66	43 % = 0.43	67.1 % = 0.671
131 % = 1.31	98.9 % = 0.989	81 % = 0.81
144 % = 1.44	64.3 % = 0.643	6 % = 0.06
24 % = 0.24	52.6 % = 0.526	17 % = 0.17

Convert Percent to Fraction

$123 \% = \frac{123}{100}$ $\qquad$ $49 \% = \frac{49}{100}$ $\qquad$ $107 \% = \frac{107}{100}$

$47.1 \% = \frac{471}{1000}$ $\qquad$ $111 \% = \frac{111}{100}$ $\qquad$ $132 \% = \frac{132}{100} = \frac{33}{25}$

$64.2 \% = \frac{642}{1000} = \frac{321}{500}$ $\qquad$ $17.4 \% = \frac{174}{1000} = \frac{87}{500}$ $\qquad$ $108 \% = \frac{108}{100} = \frac{27}{25}$

$63 \% = \frac{63}{100}$ $\qquad$ $67 \% = \frac{67}{100}$ $\qquad$ $194 \% = \frac{194}{100} = \frac{97}{50}$

$125 \% = \frac{125}{100} = \frac{5}{4}$ $\qquad$ $52.5 \% = \frac{525}{1000} = \frac{21}{40}$ $\qquad$ $12.5 \% = \frac{125}{1000} = \frac{1}{8}$

Professor Zach's Percentage Conversion Practice

III

1	3	3	6	3
+ 5	+ 3	+ 9	+ 2	+ 2

2	7	8	9	7
+ 3	+ 8	+ 1	+ 9	+ 5

6	5	2	7	0
+ 6	+ 4	+ 4	+ 2	+ 2

Professor Zach's Single Digit Addition Practice

$$\begin{array}{r} 1 \\ + 5 \\ \hline 6 \end{array} \qquad \begin{array}{r} 3 \\ + 3 \\ \hline 6 \end{array} \qquad \begin{array}{r} 3 \\ + 9 \\ \hline 12 \end{array} \qquad \begin{array}{r} 6 \\ + 2 \\ \hline 8 \end{array} \qquad \begin{array}{r} 3 \\ + 2 \\ \hline 5 \end{array}$$

$$\begin{array}{r} 2 \\ + 3 \\ \hline 5 \end{array} \qquad \begin{array}{r} 7 \\ + 8 \\ \hline 15 \end{array} \qquad \begin{array}{r} 8 \\ + 1 \\ \hline 9 \end{array} \qquad \begin{array}{r} 9 \\ + 9 \\ \hline 18 \end{array} \qquad \begin{array}{r} 7 \\ + 5 \\ \hline 12 \end{array}$$

$$\begin{array}{r} 6 \\ + 6 \\ \hline 12 \end{array} \qquad \begin{array}{r} 5 \\ + 4 \\ \hline 9 \end{array} \qquad \begin{array}{r} 2 \\ + 4 \\ \hline 6 \end{array} \qquad \begin{array}{r} 7 \\ + 2 \\ \hline 9 \end{array} \qquad \begin{array}{r} 0 \\ + 2 \\ \hline 2 \end{array}$$

Professor Zach's Single Digit Addition Practice

$99 \div 9 =$ $48 \div 4 =$ $36 \div 6 =$ $50 \div 5 =$

$120 \div 12 =$ $35 \div 7 =$ $2 \div 1 =$ $9 \div 3 =$

$28 \div 7 =$ $70 \div 10 =$ $16 \div 4 =$ $21 \div 3 =$

$96 \div 12 =$ $8 \div 8 =$ $50 \div 10 =$ $6 \div 6 =$

$15 \div 5 =$ $18 \div 2 =$ $22 \div 11 =$ $121 \div 11 =$

Professor Zach's Single Digit Division Practice

$99 \div 9 = 11$ $48 \div 4 = 12$ $36 \div 6 = 6$ $50 \div 5 = 10$

$120 \div 12 = 10$ $35 \div 7 = 5$ $2 \div 1 = 2$ $9 \div 3 = 3$

$28 \div 7 = 4$ $70 \div 10 = 7$ $16 \div 4 = 4$ $21 \div 3 = 7$

$96 \div 12 = 8$ $8 \div 8 = 1$ $50 \div 10 = 5$ $6 \div 6 = 1$

$15 \div 5 = 3$ $18 \div 2 = 9$ $22 \div 11 = 2$ $121 \div 11 = 11$

Professor Zach's Single Digit Division Practice

$$9\overline{)576} \qquad 6\overline{)456} \qquad 4\overline{)280} \qquad 2\overline{)158}$$

$$9\overline{)108} \qquad 6\overline{)234} \qquad 5\overline{)55} \qquad 4\overline{)224}$$

$$5\overline{)425} \qquad 5\overline{)160} \qquad 4\overline{)380} \qquad 8\overline{)384}$$

Professor Zach's Single Digit Long Division Practice

$$9\overline{)576}\quad\frac{64}{}$$

$$6\overline{)456}\quad\frac{76}{}$$

$$4\overline{)280}\quad\frac{70}{}$$

$$2\overline{)158}\quad\frac{79}{}$$

$$9\overline{)108}\quad\frac{12}{}$$

$$6\overline{)234}\quad\frac{39}{}$$

$$5\overline{)55}\quad\frac{11}{}$$

$$4\overline{)224}\quad\frac{56}{}$$

$$5\overline{)425}\quad\frac{85}{}$$

$$5\overline{)160}\quad\frac{32}{}$$

$$4\overline{)380}\quad\frac{95}{}$$

$$8\overline{)384}\quad\frac{48}{}$$

Professor Zach's Single Digit Long Division Practice

$9\overline{)291}$ $4\overline{)86}$ $2\overline{)55}$ $7\overline{)522}$

$5\overline{)189}$ $3\overline{)151}$ $7\overline{)152}$ $2\overline{)91}$

$7\overline{)429}$ $3\overline{)178}$ $3\overline{)185}$ $8\overline{)305}$

Professor Zach's Single Digit Long Division Practice with Remainders

$$9 \overline{)291} \quad 32 \text{ r } 3$$

$$4 \overline{)86} \quad 21 \text{ r } 2$$

$$2 \overline{)55} \quad 27 \text{ r } 1$$

$$7 \overline{)522} \quad 74 \text{ r } 4$$

$$5 \overline{)189} \quad 37 \text{ r } 4$$

$$3 \overline{)151} \quad 50 \text{ r } 1$$

$$7 \overline{)152} \quad 21 \text{ r } 5$$

$$2 \overline{)91} \quad 45 \text{ r } 1$$

$$7 \overline{)429} \quad 61 \text{ r } 2$$

$$3 \overline{)178} \quad 59 \text{ r } 1$$

$$3 \overline{)185} \quad 61 \text{ r } 2$$

$$8 \overline{)305} \quad 38 \text{ r } 1$$

Professor Zach's Single Digit Long Division Practice with Remainders

4	2	1	8	9
x 4	x 6	x 8	x 3	x 8

2	5	1	1	2
x 3	x 9	x 8	x 9	x 0

2	0	4	0	4
x 4	x 3	x 0	x 1	x 8

Professor Zach's Single Digit Multiplication Practice

4	2	1	8	9
x 4	x 6	x 8	x 3	x 8
16	12	8	24	72

2	5	1	1	2
x 3	x 9	x 8	x 9	x 0
6	45	8	9	0

2	0	4	0	4
x 4	x 3	x 0	x 1	x 8
8	0	0	0	32

Professor Zach's Single Digit Multiplication Practice

$$\begin{array}{r} 9 \\ -\ 3 \\ \hline \end{array} \qquad \begin{array}{r} 8 \\ -\ 3 \\ \hline \end{array} \qquad \begin{array}{r} 7 \\ -\ 0 \\ \hline \end{array} \qquad \begin{array}{r} 7 \\ -\ 6 \\ \hline \end{array} \qquad \begin{array}{r} 9 \\ -\ 7 \\ \hline \end{array}$$

$$\begin{array}{r} 6 \\ -\ 5 \\ \hline \end{array} \qquad \begin{array}{r} 7 \\ -\ 3 \\ \hline \end{array} \qquad \begin{array}{r} 9 \\ -\ 5 \\ \hline \end{array} \qquad \begin{array}{r} 6 \\ -\ 1 \\ \hline \end{array} \qquad \begin{array}{r} 9 \\ -\ 1 \\ \hline \end{array}$$

$$\begin{array}{r} 6 \\ -\ 4 \\ \hline \end{array} \qquad \begin{array}{r} 8 \\ -\ 8 \\ \hline \end{array} \qquad \begin{array}{r} 3 \\ -\ 1 \\ \hline \end{array} \qquad \begin{array}{r} 7 \\ -\ 2 \\ \hline \end{array} \qquad \begin{array}{r} 6 \\ -\ 4 \\ \hline \end{array}$$

Professor Zach's Single Digit Subtraction Practice

```
   9        8        7        7        9
 - 3      - 3      - 0      - 6      - 7
 ___      ___      ___      ___      ___
   6        5        7        1        2
```

```
   6        7        9        6        9
 - 5      - 3      - 5      - 1      - 1
 ___      ___      ___      ___      ___
   1        4        4        5        8
```

```
   6        8        3        7        6
 - 4      - 8      - 1      - 2      - 4
 ___      ___      ___      ___      ___
   2        0        2        5        2
```

Professor Zach's Single Digit Subtraction Practice

Converting Fahrenheit and Celsius

Convert Fahrenheit to Celsius $C = \frac{5}{9} \times (F - 32)$

1) $89^\circ F$ _____   5) $109^\circ F$ _____

2) $32^\circ F$ _____   6) $65^\circ F$ _____

3) $60^\circ F$ _____   7) $103^\circ F$ _____

4) $69^\circ F$ _____   8) $58^\circ F$ _____

Convert Celsius to Fahrenheit $F = (\frac{9}{5} \times C) + 32$

9) $43^\circ C$ _____   13) $31^\circ C$ _____

10) $16^\circ C$ _____   14) $20^\circ C$ _____

11) $47^\circ C$ _____   15) $44^\circ C$ _____

12) $8^\circ C$ _____   16) $42^\circ C$ _____

Professor Zach's Temperature Conversion Practice

Converting Fahrenheit and Celsius

Convert Fahrenheit to Celsius $C = \frac{5}{9} \times (F - 32)$

1) $89°F$ $31.7°C$

2) $32°F$ $0.0°C$

3) $60°F$ $15.6°C$

4) $69°F$ $20.6°C$

5) $109°F$ $42.8°C$

6) $65°F$ $18.3°C$

7) $103°F$ $39.4°C$

8) $58°F$ $14.4°C$

Convert Celsius to Fahrenheit $F = (\frac{9}{5} \times C) + 32$

9) $43°C$ $109.4°F$

10) $16°C$ $60.8°F$

11) $47°C$ $116.6°F$

12) $8°C$ $46.4°F$

13) $31°C$ $87.8°F$

14) $20°C$ $68.0°F$

15) $44°C$ $111.2°F$

16) $42°C$ $107.6°F$

Professor Zach's Temperature Conversion Practice

1) 12 Months = 1 _____

2) 24 Hours = _____ Day

3) 12 _____ = 1 Year

4) _____ Minute = 60 Seconds

5) 60 Seconds = _____ Minute

6) 12 Months = _____ Year

7) _____ Seconds = 1 Minute

8) 365 _____ = 1 Year

9) 60 Minutes = _____ Hour

10) _____ Minute = 60 Seconds

11) _____ Hours = 1 Day

12) 7 Days = _____ Week

13) 24 Hours = 1 _____

14) 30 _____ = 1/2 Hour

15) 60 Seconds = 1 _____

16) 60 Minutes = 1 _____

17) _____ Hours = 1 Day

18) 24 Hours = 1 _____

19) 12 _____ = 1 Year

20) 15 Minutes = _____ Hour

Professor Zach's Time Conversion Practice

1) 12 Months = 1 Year

2) 24 Hours = 1 Day

3) 12 Months = 1 Year

4) 1 Minute = 60 Seconds

5) 60 Seconds = 1 Minute

6) 12 Months = 1 Year

7) 60 Seconds = 1 Minute

8) 365 Days = 1 Year

9) 60 Minutes = 1 Hour

10) 1 Minute = 60 Seconds

11) 24 Hours = 1 Day

12) 7 Days = 1 Week

13) 24 Hours = 1 Day

14) 30 Minutes = 1/2 Hour

15) 60 Seconds = 1 Minute

16) 60 Minutes = 1 Hour

17) 24 Hours = 1 Day

18) 24 Hours = 1 Day

19) 12 Months = 1 Year

20) 15 Minutes = 1/4 Hour

Professor Zach's Time Conversion Practice

Name : _____   Score : _____

Teacher : _____   Date : _____

996	762	365	315	904
+ 504	+ 238	+ 741	+ 227	+ 676

509	342	578	819	989
+ 457	+ 595	+ 813	+ 913	+ 775

498	526	343	490	944
+ 755	+ 790	+ 916	+ 536	+ 361

Professor Zach's Triple Digit Addition Practice

996	762	365	315	904
+ 504	+ 238	+ 741	+ 227	+ 676
1500	1000	1106	542	1580

509	342	578	819	989
+ 457	+ 595	+ 813	+ 913	+ 775
966	937	1391	1732	1764

498	526	343	490	944
+ 755	+ 790	+ 916	+ 536	+ 361
1253	1316	1259	1026	1305

Professor Zach's Triple Digit Addition Practice

695	765	801	620	994
- 580	- 554	- 330	- 561	- 741

577	647	764	955	310
- 124	- 225	- 196	- 590	- 301

722	846	684	991	560
- 293	- 274	- 146	- 934	- 518

Professor Zach's Triple Digit Subtraction Practice

```
  695        765        801        620        994
- 580      - 554      - 330      - 561      - 741
-----      -----      -----      -----      -----
  115        211        471         59        253


  577        647        764        955        310
- 124      - 225      - 196      - 590      - 301
-----      -----      -----      -----      -----
  453        422        568        365          9


  722        846        684        991        560
- 293      - 274      - 146      - 934      - 518
-----      -----      -----      -----      -----
  429        572        538         57         42
```

Professor Zach's Triple Digit Subtraction Practice

ضافی

سیکھنے کے مقاصد

طلباء کو طلباء کو دو بندشوں میں شامل کرنے کے قابل ہو جائے گا

تعارف

علموں کے سلینڈ دو پر دکھائی بورڈ طالب
بورڈ پر آسان عروض ڈرائیو دوگاڑیوں کو ایک گروپ کے طور پر آپ طور
پر نشان زد کرنا اور سنگل کار گروپ کے طور پر اس کے آگے ایک اور
اور سنگھ سنگی کا گروپ کے طور پر اس کے آگے ایک اور ایک کو اپنی
طرف متوجہ کریں جس کے نتیجے میں دونوں گروپوں کو مل کر دکھایا گیا
ہے

تین کاری مل کر تین کریں مل کر تین کاری مل کر طلبہ سے ان کا شمار کرنے
کے لئے چوک پرچی طلباء سے جوابات لی درست جوابات کو ظاہر کرنے کی
کرتے ہیں اور اس کے علاوہ عمل کی وضاحت کرتے ہیں

ہدایت کی مشق

طلباء کو ایک اضافی ورکشاپ دیا جائے گا اور کلاس سب سے پہلے کریں گے
بائی کوٹ روڈ پر ایک ساتھ مسئلہ عکاسی کا استعمال کرتے ہوئے اساتذہ استاد
کو شیٹ کے مسائل سے متعلق بات چیت کرے گی

آزاد کام

طلباء چھوٹے گروپوں میں کام کریں گے اور کشمش سے مساوات کو حل
کرنے میں جب طالبعلم واحد اکاؤنٹس کے علاوہ ماسٹر مالک ہوتے ہیں تو ڈبل
اور ٹرپل ڈاکٹر اضافی ہوجائیگا متعارف کرایا علاوہ کا استعمال کرتے ہوئے
انہیں سکھانے کے لئے ایک طریقہ کے طور پر

ذات سکھانے کے مقاصد طلباء کو دو ہندسوں کو کم کرنے کے قابل ہو جائے
گا تعارف دربا طالب علم کو سلینڈ بارہ پر ڈیگرام دکھائی کینیڈی کے دو

گروپوں کی ایک تاریک ڈرامہ 2

دو کے برابر ہونے کے بجائے ان کے درمیان ایک چھوٹا سا نشان لگائیں کم
کرنے کی وضاحت کرنا ہر طرف سے ہر طرف سے کنڈی کا ایک ٹکڑا پارکر
کے جس کا رخ صفر تک پہنچ جاتا ہے اس لینڈ 13 کی نمبر لائن کو مزید
وضاحت کرنے کے لئے استعمال کریں کہ چار کی اصل قیمت کس طرح ہے
دو کی طرف سے کمی

ہدایات کی مشق طلبہ کو ذیلی ذرا کاری ورکاں دیا جائے گا اور کلاس پہلے
کریں گے بورڈ پر ایک دوسرے کے ساتھ مسلح کی عکاسی کا استعمال کرتے
ہوئے اساتذہ کو ورکشاپ سے مسئلہ سے متعلق مسائل کا سامنا کرنا پڑتا ہے

سلیم ٹشو سے مسئلہ

آزاد کام طلباء چھوٹے گروپوں میں کام کریں گے ورکشاپس وقت سے مساوات
کو حل کرنے میں طالبعلموں کو واحد اکاؤنٹس کے حصول کا مالک ہونے کے
بعد ڈبل اور ٹرپل

ذرا سی سراب سکھانے کے مقاصد طلبہ کو دو بندوں میں مندوں کو جذب
کرنے کے قابل ہو جائے گا تعارف سلینڈ بیس پر طالب علموں کی تصویر
دکھائی 21 پر دکھائے گا دکھایا گیا ہے کے طور پر اس کا بار بار اضافی طور
پر ظاہر ہوتا ہے اسی گروپ کاری کا طریقہ استعمال کریں جو وضاحت کرنے
کے لئے اضافی سبق میں استعمال کیا جاتا تھا یہ حقیقت ہے کیا طالب علموں کو
دوبارہ باربار اضافی طریقہ استعمال کرنا ہے جب تک کہ وہ آرام دے ہو

ضرب جنرلوں کو یاد رکھنے کے ساتھ ہدایت کی مشق اساتذہ کو ظاہر کرتا ہے
جیسے کلاس کچھ مسائل کے ذریعے کام کرے گی اضافی باربار ہے

آزاد کام

الابہا واحد عددی اور ضرب کاری ورکشاپ کے ذریعے جائیں گے استعمال کرتے ہوئے اہمیت کے بعد ضرب کو سمجھنے کے لئے ابتدا طور پر باربار اضافی طریقہ

عملی طور پر طالب علموں کو بجائے اضافی استعمال کے بجائے ضرب کرنے کی کوشش کرنا ہے ان کی سٹیک ریاضی میں ضرب کی علامت کا استعمال کرتے ہوئے

ڈویژن سکھانے کے مقاصد طلباء کو دو ہندسوں کو تقسیم کرنے کے قابل ہو جائے گا تعارف طالب علموں کو سلینڈر پر مسئلہ دکھائیں یہ بتائیں کہ زیورات کس طرح یہی تین آثار قدیمہ کے درمیان تقسیم کیا گیا ہے سلینڈ 32 پر مستقل کریں منتقل کریں 23 کے اعداد و شمار کے ساتھ اسی منظر میں بیان کریں اور وضاحت کریں باقی کیسے کام کرتے ہیں ہدایت کی مشق طلباء کو ایک ڈویژن ورکشاپس دیا جائے گا اور اس طرح طریقوں کو ملازمت ملے گی مسائل کو حل کریں کافی مشقت ڈویژن کا طریقہ کار نافذ کیا جائے گا آزاد کام

طلبہ کو چھوٹے گروہوں میں تقسیم کریں گے ابتدا طور پہ دکھائے گا طریقہ استعمال کرتے ہوئے سلینڈ 33 پر اور آخر میں طویل ڈویژن کا استعمال کرتے ہوئے

کمان سکھانے کے مقاصد

سوئس اور ہزارہ جگہ جگہ ہو کے بارے میں سیکھیں گے اعدادوشمار کے ساتھ اضافی اضافی ذات ضرب اور تقسیم کو لاگو کرنا ہے فیصلہ

فیصلہ

تعارف

طالبعلم کی تصویر سلینڈر چالیس پر دکھائی وضاحت کریں کہ کس طرح ڈیولپمنٹ پوری طرح کا حصہ ہیں کہ سلینڈ پر جاری رکھیں ڈیولپمنٹ کی تشریح بیان کریں ہدایت کی ماش سلینڈ 41 پر دشواری کے ذریعے کام کریں کہ اس کے حساب سے اس کا مطلب ہے اس طرح کا کارروائیاں پوری تعداد میں

ہیں آزاد کام طلباء کو اضافی ذات ضرب اور تقسیم پر کام کرے گا ورزش کو اعتماد پیدا کرنے کے لیے جو پہلے سے طے شدہ طریقوں کو ملازمہ کرتی ہیں وہ ایک ہے قابل عمل حکمت عملی

سکھانے کے مقاصد طلباء اس بات کا تعین کرنے کے لئے سیکھیں گے کہ مختلف ٹرانزیکشنز کا منافع بخش کیا ہوگا یا نقصان یا خالص نقصان نفس خالص منافع

تعارف

سلینڈر 45 اور اڑتالیس پر مسائل کے ذریعے کام کریں گے طالب علموں کو کیسے دکھایا گیا ہے اس بات کا تعین کریں ہے خالص فائدہ یا نقصان خالد نقصان ہدایت کی مشق طالبعلموں کو خشک کرنے کے لیے ذات کے استعمال سے مشق سے مسائل کے ذریعے کام کریں گے

جواب دیں یہ بتائیں کہ خالص منافع یا خالص نقصان آخر نتیجہ تھا آزاد کام طلبہ پہلے استعمال کرتے ہوئے منافع یا نقصان کے مسائل کے ایک ورک کے ذریعے کام کریں گے پہلے بیان کردہ طریقوں پر یہ بتایاگیا

فیصد

سیکھنے کے مقصد طلباء فیصد کے بارے میں سیکھیں گے تعارف سلینڈ ترین پر مسلح کے ذریعے کام کریں گے طلباء کی مدد کے لیے سلینڈ 57 پر گرافکس کا استعمال کریں گے کہ کتنے فیصد ہیں اور 56 دکھاکر فیصد پر فیصد سے متعلق ہدایت کی مشق طالب علموں کو ڈیویژن اور ظرف کا استعمال کرتے ہوئے مشکے مسائل کے ذریعے کام کریں گے اور 56 پر دکھائی دکھایا گیا ہے

آزاد کا

طلبہ تلوار چھوٹے گروپوں میں مسائل کے ذریعے کام کریں گے مساوات کو حل کرنے سے حل کریں گے ورکشاپ پیمائش کی اکائیاں سیکھنے کے مقاصد طلباء وزن وقت درجہ حرارت اور پیمائش کی پیمائش کے بارے میں سیکھیں گے فاصلے تعارف طلباء کا مشاہدہ کریں گے

لجبرا ہدایت کی ماش

سیاہ سوال کے نشان جیسے نشان ابتدائی طور پر مسائل میں استعمال back

کیسے کیے جاسکتے ہیں کہ طالب علموں کو لاپتہ یا نامعلوم کی تصور کو
آسانی سے سمجھا جاسکتا ہے

بدر بلآخر طلبہ کو اس علامت کو ایکس کے ساتھ تبدیل کرنا چاہیے یہ نہیں قائم
کرے گا زیادہ آزاد جدید کام طلباء چھوٹے گروپ میں مسائل کے ذریعے کام
کریں گے مساوات کو حل کرنے کسے حل کریں گے ورکشاپ

جیومیٹری سیکھنے کے مقاصد

طلباء جامعاتی کے بارے میں سیکھیں گے اور مختلف سائز کیسے بیان کی
جائیگی تعارف طلباء کی بنیاد پر مختلف سائزوں کی شناخت پر مشتمل ہوگی
خصوصیات ہدایت کی مشق

طلباء کو مختلف قسم کے مختلف سائز استاد کی طرف سے تیار کردہ دکھایا
جائے گا دکھایا گیا ہے استاد اس جوابات کو ظاہر کرے گا اور وضاحت کرے
گا کہ ہم کس طرح سمجھتے ہیں کونسا سیکشن پر مشکل میں فٹ بیٹھتا ہے آزاد
کام یہ ایک گروپ مشک ہوگیا لہذا کوئی آزاد کام موجود نہ ہو

گرافک

سیکھنے کے مقاصد طلباء گرافکس لین دین مساوات کے بارے میں سیکھیں
گے تعارف وضاحت کی جائے گی اس لینڈ 77 اسی کا استعمال کرتے ہوئے
کس طرح لکیر کو ظاہر کرنے کے لئے ایک

مسا مساوات انگور ہی ہدایت کی مشق

استاد کسی کسی گراف کو ڈھانچے اور کسی لائن یا مساوات کا استعمال
کرسکتے ہیں پوچھیں طالب علم کسی دوسرے نصف کا تعین کرنے کے
لئے آزاد کام طلباء چھوٹے گروپ میں مسائل کے ذریعے کام کریں گے
مساوات کو حل کرنے سے حل کریں گے

Printed in the United States
By Bookmasters